Frogs

by Tara Stern

Bullfrog

Companion to **The Troll in the Creek**

Bullfrog

A frog is a small animal.
Most frogs live near water.
They live near ponds, lakes,
streams, and swamps.

Tree frog

Some frogs live in trees. Tree frogs have sticky pads on their feet. The sticky pads help them climb trees.

Frogs have short front legs.
Their front legs prop them up
when they sit.

Frogs have long back legs.
These legs help them jump.
Frogs can jump high and far.

Frogs also use their legs to swim.
The web of skin between
their toes helps them swim.

Bullfrog

Frogs have big eyes on top of their heads. They use their eyes to look for food. They watch for danger.

Green frog

Frogs have long tongues.
A frog can flip out its
tongue and catch a meal.

8

Frogs eat insects, spiders,
worms, and slugs.
They swallow their food whole.

Frogs lay their eggs in water.

Each egg hatches into a tadpole.

The tadpole grows legs.
Its tail gets shorter.

Then the tadpole becomes a frog.

Spring peeper

Wood frog

Bullfrog

Some frogs croak.
Some frogs peep.
What sounds do you think
these frogs make?